My Boudoir Experience

A Captivating Journey of Love through Boudoir

S. M. Bikanu

Copyright © S. M. bikanu 2023

All rights reserved. This eBook or any portion thereof may not be reproduced or used in any manner whatsoever without the express written permission of the author except for the use of brief quotations in a book review.

This is a work of fiction. Names, characters, organizations, places, events, and incidents are either products of the author's imagination or used fictitiously.

All rights reserved

Blurb

I was looking for a boudoir photographer, but I got more than I asked for.

In "My Boudoir Experience," embark on a mesmerizing tale of unexpected passion, self-discovery, and the transformative power of love. Nivedita, a bride-to-be on the brink of matrimony, finds herself drawn into a whirlwind of emotions when she contacts renowned boudoir photographer, Sahil, for a bridal photoshoot. Little does she know that this fateful decision will unravel a chain of events that will forever alter the course of her life.

As the camera captures Nivedita's beauty, vulnerability, and unspoken desires, a palpable connection ignites between her and Sahil. With each click of the shutter, the invisible walls surrounding their hearts crumble, allowing a forbidden intimacy to flourish. Bound by their shared passion and an unyielding pull toward one another, they find solace and liberation in the depths of their desires.

As Nivedita navigates the final week leading up to her wedding, she becomes entangled in a tempest of emotions—a maelstrom of devotion, guilt, and the stirring realization that her heart may belong to another. The lines between duty, tradition, and personal fulfilment blur, and she is faced with a profound choice that could either shatter or redefine her future.

In the midst of this emotional turbulence, "My Boudoir Experience" explores themes of self-discovery, societal expectations, and the courage to follow one's heart. Nivedita's journey unfolds with sensuality and raw vulnerability, as she grapples with her own desires while grappling with the consequences of her actions.

Will Nivedita choose the path paved by convention and duty, honouring the commitment she made to her fiancé? Or will she embrace the intoxicating allure of newfound love, risking everything she holds dear for a chance at true happiness?

This captivating story, "My Boudoir Experience" takes readers on an exploration of love's complexity, unveiling the depths of passion, the power of personal choice, and the indomitable nature of the human spirit. With its evocative prose, rich character development, and an exquisite blend of sensuality and emotional resonance, this tale invites readers to confront their own desires, question societal norms, and ultimately, believe in the transformative power of love.

Contents

My Boudoir Experience 1

Blurb 3

Contents 6

Chapter 1 – Embracing My Inner Vixen ... 8

Chapter 2 - Boudoir Passion 16

Chapter 3 – Unleashing My Sensuality .. 23

Chapter 4 – A Captivating Encounter 29

Chapter 5 – Capturing My Essence 33

Chapter 6 – The Boudoir Shoot 37

Chapter 7 - A Tense Conversation 47

Chapter 8 – Tension in the Air 55

Chapter 9 – Unveiling Shadows 58

Chapter 10 – The Serendipity 66

Chapter 1 – Embracing My Inner Vixen

Nivedita's POV

I am getting married, and there is one thing that I want to do more than even the bachelorette party—Boudoir photography.

Remember that Bollywood song in which Nora Fatehi says:

Kal meri shaadi hai...

Aaj aazadi hai...

And she celebrates it by grooving to the popular item song:

Ek to kam zindagani

Well, I don't want to go and dance in the midst of a gang of men, but I want to do an elaborate photo session.

For sure…

In the realm of verses, let my desires unfurl,

As a woman, bold and free, my spirit will swirl.

With grace and strength, I claim my rightful space,

To live a life on my terms, in captivating embrace.

In the quiet whispers of the moonlit night,

I yearn for liberation, to bask in my own light.

No longer confined by society's narrow view,

I celebrate my sensuality, both daring and true.

Oh, how I crave to dance upon life's grand stage,

To revel in pleasures, unburdened by age.

I'll shatter expectations, break through each mould,

Embracing my passions, unapologetically bold.

No longer restrained by judgments, or society's chains,

I'll paint my canvas with desires that flow through my veins.

Through subtle gestures and a fiery gaze,

I'll weave tales of allure in this captivating maze.

In the whispers of the wind, I find my solace,

A melody of freedom, a symphony of promise.

I'll savour every moment, each breath, and touch,

Embracing my femininity, for it is mine to clutch.

No longer shall I wilt beneath conventions' weight,

For I am a woman, and I choose my own fate.

In this life I shall flourish, vibrant and free,

Celebrating my sensuality with unbridled glee.

So raise a glass to the audacity within my soul,

To the woman unafraid to claim what's hers, whole.

Let my poetry be a testament, an anthem to proclaim,

That I shall live my life on my terms, unshackled from shame.

I learned about boudoir photography from a random comedy podcast I was watching on YouTube. I just knew I had to do it.

At least once.

So, here I am, on the brink of matrimonial bliss, eagerly planning for the big day. As the wedding bells draw near, my mind races with a whirlwind of thoughts. Who will catch the bouquet? Will Uncle Joe break out his questionable dance moves again? And, most importantly, how can I make this once-in-a-lifetime experience unforgettable?

Sure, there's the usual bachelorette party shenanigans, complete with tiaras, feather boas, and an abundance of questionable decisions. But amidst the raucous laughter and wild escapades, there's one thing that occupies my mind more than anything else: boudoir photography.

Now, you might be thinking, "Boudoir photography? Isn't that just a fancy way of saying you want to pose in your underwear for a camera?"

Well, my friend, let me tell you, it's so much more than that. It's an artistic form—a way to capture the essence of my womanhood and celebrate the confidence that lies within.

Believe it or not, my introduction to the enchanting world of boudoir photography came from an unexpected source—a random comedy podcast I stumbled upon while mindlessly scrolling through YouTube. Who would've thought that amidst the jokes and laughter, I'd discover something that would ignite a spark within me?

The podcast hosts, with their witty banter and infectious humour, regaled tales of boudoir sessions gone wrong and the empowering stories of women who dared to embrace their sensuality. It was like stumbling upon a hidden treasure chest filled with sparkling jewels of self-expression and unabashed confidence.

Intrigued, I delved deeper into the art form, immersing myself in a sea of stunning images that showcased the raw beauty of women in all their glory. I saw the allure in the shadows and the captivating power of vulnerability. Suddenly, the idea of boudoir photography became more than just a fleeting fancy—it became a must-do before saying "I do."

Now, some may raise an eyebrow and ask, "Why go through all this trouble? Isn't the wedding day itself enough?" Oh, dear reader, let me enlighten you. Boudoir photography is not merely about capturing pretty pictures; it's about tapping into a side of me that often goes unnoticed in the hustle and bustle of everyday life.

It's about embracing my inner vixen, unabashedly flaunting my curves, and celebrating my body as a work of art. It's a chance to be the leading lady of my own seductive photo shoot, a starring role that allows me to unleash my playful spirit and bask in the spotlight.

You see, boudoir photography isn't just about the tantalizing visuals—it's about capturing the very essence of my femininity. It's about embracing my curves, my quirks, and all the little imperfections that make me uniquely me. In a world that often tries to dictate what beauty should look like, boudoir photography allows me to redefine beauty on my own terms.

There's a certain magic that happens when you step into that studio, surrounded by soft lighting and an atmosphere that feels like pure enchantment. It's like being transported to a world where confidence reigns supreme, where vulnerability is celebrated, and where every curve is seen as a stroke of artistic brilliance.

With each click of the camera, I'm reminded that beauty comes in all shapes and sizes. It's not about conforming to societal standards; it's about embracing the goddess within and letting her shine through. Boudoir photography has a way of capturing that ethereal glow, that twinkle in the eye that says, "I am fierce, and I am unapologetically me."

And let's not forget the journey of self-discovery that comes along with it. Through boudoir photography, I've learned to love and appreciate my body in ways I never thought possible. It's like gazing into a mirror and seeing a version of myself that is unafraid to be seen, unafraid to own her sensuality, and unafraid to revel in her own skin.

It's empowering, really, to have a tangible reminder of the beauty that lies within. A boudoir photograph is more than just a snapshot; it's a piece of art that captures a moment frozen in time—a moment where I am unapologetically radiant, confident, and fiercely feminine.

And let's not forget the exhilaration that comes with the big reveal. Picture this: surrounded by friends, champagne in hand, as I unveil my boudoir album. The gasps, the applause, the sheer awe on their faces—it's a testament to the transformative power of boudoir photography.

So, as I walk down the aisle, my heart filled with love and anticipation, I'll carry with me the memory of those breath-taking boudoir images. They will serve as a reminder of the journey I took, the woman I became, and the unbreakable spirit that will forever be a part of me.

Boudoir photography, my dear friend, is so much more than just an artistic form. It's a celebration of self, a reclaiming of femininity, and a powerful statement of confidence. It's a way to honour the woman I am today and the woman I will continue to evolve into. And in this chapter of my life, as I embark on the adventure of marriage, there's nothing quite like boudoir photography to remind me that the most beautiful love story begins with the love I have for myself.

So, armed with my newfound knowledge and a spirit of adventure, I embarked on a quest to find the perfect boudoir photographer. Armed with my lacy lingerie, killer heels, and a heart full of anticipation, I'm ready to capture the essence of this transformative journey.

I may be on the precipice of marital bliss, but before I embark on that journey, I want to celebrate the woman I am right now. Boudoir photography—it's like a love letter to myself, a reminder that I am beautiful, confident, and worthy of admiration.

As the camera clicks and the lens captures my essence, I will savour every moment, relishing in the knowledge that I am not just a bride-to-be but a woman stepping into her own power. So here's to boudoir photography—a witty and whimsical adventure that promises to uncover a side of me I never knew existed.

As I scroll through the profiles of countless boudoir photographers, one name jumps out at me like a sizzling spark: Sahil. Intriguing and captivating, his portfolio pulls me deeper into the visual realm he has created. And boy, am I in for a treat!

Picture this: a black-and-white photograph, bathed in soft, moody lighting. The composition is sheer perfection—a play of light and shadows, sculpting every contour of the subject's body. It's sensuous, yet elegant. In that single frame, Sahil captures the essence of feminine grace and mystique. It's like stepping into a classic film noir, where every glance, every curve, holds a story waiting to be unravelled.

And then, there's the photograph of a woman reclining on a plush velvet chaise, her eyes fixed upon an unseen horizon. The backdrop, a vintage boudoir with fringed lampshades and delicate lace curtains, adds a touch of nostalgic romance. Sahil's meticulous attention to detail is evident in every element—the way the light caresses her face, the gentle curve of her lips, and the dainty arch of her back. It's a portrait that whispers tales of vulnerability and strength, encapsulating the complex layers of womanhood.

But my personal favourite has to be the photograph of a woman standing tall, her body adorned in delicate lingerie, with her tousled hair cascading down her back. In this image, Sahil captures an exquisite blend of confidence and vulnerability. Her gaze pierces through the lens, a magnetic pull that draws me into her world. It's a moment frozen in time, where the essence of empowerment dances harmoniously with raw, unapologetic sensuality.

What sets Sahil's photographs apart is his ability to capture the unguarded moments—the subtle nuances that make a woman beautifully human. Each image he crafts seems to transcend the confines of a mere photograph, becoming a portal to a realm where fantasy and reality intertwine. It's as if Sahil possesses a magical lens that reveals the truest version of his subjects—their strengths, their desires, and their inherent beauty.

As I envision myself in front of Sahil's camera, I can't help but feel a surge of excitement. His artistry ignites a flame within me, a burning desire to step into my own power and celebrate my femininity like never before. Sahil's photographs promise to capture not just the external beauty but the essence of my being—an unapologetic celebration of all that makes me who I am.

With his keen eye for detail and an uncanny ability to capture the essence of womanhood, Sahil becomes more than a photographer in my eyes. He's a storyteller, an artist, and a visionary who can transform an ordinary moment into an extraordinary work of art. And with each click of his camera, I know that my boudoir experience will be nothing short of extraordinary— a journey that forever etches my story onto the canvas of his lens.

I just knew whom to contact.

Chapter 2 - Boudoir Passion

Sahil's POV

I'm a Boudoir photographer, unabashedly, unashamedly.

It's very difficult to not be affected by the whispers around me, but I have developed a thick skin about it.

Boudoir is an art form very few appreciate. It's a delicate dance between sensuality and vulnerability, capturing the essence of a woman in her most intimate moments. How did I stumble upon this captivating world, you ask? Well, let me take you back to the early days of my career when passion and necessity collided.

Back then, I was a struggling photographer, hustling to make ends meet. Desperate for some quick cash, I found myself agreeing to do a boudoir session. Little did I know that this seemingly mundane decision would ignite a fire within me—a passion that would shape my artistic journey.

As I entered that dimly lit room, camera in hand, I had no idea what to expect. My client, a bold fashion, model had already done a boudoir session before, and had more experience than me. She knew how to pose, and even about the lighting and angles. All I had to do was to click. But as soon as the shutter clicked, something magical happened. In that moment, I realized the power of boudoir photography—the way it captures raw emotion celebrates femininity, and embraces every curve and flaw.

I never looked back since.

Boudoir became my obsession, my quirky passion that most people couldn't quite understand. While others dismissed it as mere titillation, I saw it as an opportunity to create art that spoke volumes. It was a chance to empower women, to help them discover newfound confidence and see themselves in a way they had never imagined.

In the beginning, I faced my fair share of sceptics and critics. But their doubts only fuelled my determination. I dove headfirst into mastering the art of boudoir photography, honing my skills and embracing the beauty in every frame. I studied the interplay of light and shadow, the art of posing, and the delicate balance between intimacy and artistry.

Through countless boudoir sessions, I witnessed the transformative power it held. I saw women shed their inhibitions, letting their inner vixen emerge with grace and unapologetic confidence. It was a privilege to be a part of their journey, capturing their stories through the lens of my camera.

Boudoir photography, for me, is a celebration of vulnerability. It's about creating a safe space where women can explore their sensuality, free from judgment or societal expectations. It's not just about capturing alluring images—it's about revealing the layers of strength and beauty that lie beneath the surface.

Every session is a collaboration—a dance between photographer and muse. I strive to create an atmosphere of trust, where my subjects can let go and truly be themselves. Together, we unravel the intricacies of their personalities, their desires, and their unique brand of beauty.

So, as I continue on this passionate journey, I am grateful for that one fateful boudoir session that changed the course of my career. Boudoir photography is not just my job; it's my calling—a form of art that allows me to capture the raw emotions and unapologetic sensuality of women in their most intimate moments.

Every time I click the shutter, freezing those captivating moments in time, I am reminded of the profound impact boudoir photography has on both the subject and the artist. It's a testament to the human spirit, an ode to self-love and empowerment. Through my lens, I strive to share this unique perspective with the world—one captivating image at a time.

I live by three rules:

1. Never be aroused while doing the shoot.
2. Never be tempted to make out with the client.
3. Be selective in taking up a client.

Some might scoff at my rules, but I live by them.

Even though I reject more contracts than I accept, my reputation in the world of boudoir photography has grown steadily. I take my work incredibly seriously, striving to create art that transcends expectations and leaves a lasting impact. It's this unwavering dedication that has led me to invest in a plush bungalow—a dedicated space that embodies the essence of a boudoir.

My studio is more than just a room with four walls: it's a sanctuary of sensuality and empowerment. As soon as you step through the door, you're enveloped in an atmosphere of elegance and intimacy. Soft, diffused lighting casts a gentle glow, while luxurious fabrics drape gracefully from every corner. It's a space meticulously designed to evoke a sense of comfort and serenity—a place where inhibitions are shed, and true beauty can flourish.

Every detail has been carefully considered to create the perfect backdrop for boudoir photography. Plush velvet chaises invite my clients to recline with confidence, while delicate lace curtains filter the light, adding an ethereal touch. Mirrors strategically placed capture tantalizing reflections, amplifying the allure of each composition.

Within these walls, I have built a haven for self-expression—a space where women can embrace their bodies, celebrate their sensuality, and explore the depths of their desires. It's a collaborative experience, with my clients and I working hand-in-hand to bring their visions to life. We experiment with different poses, angles, and moods, striving to capture the essence of their unique beauty.

My plush bungalow serves as a sanctuary for self-discovery and empowerment. It's a place where my clients can shed their inhibitions, reveal their vulnerabilities, and emerge stronger, more confident versions of themselves. It's an honour to witness this transformation and to have a space that facilitates such growth.

As I step into my studio each day, I am reminded of the profound impact boudoir photography has on the lives of those who dare to embrace it. It's not just about creating stunning images—it's about providing a safe space for women to explore their sensuality, rediscover their inner strength, and embrace their individuality.

So, within these plush walls, I pour my heart and soul into every shot, every click of the camera. I strive to capture the true essence of the boudoir—the celebration of femininity, the beauty of vulnerability, and the power of self-love. My studio is a testament to my unwavering commitment to this art form—a commitment that ensures every client who walks through those doors leaves feeling transformed, empowered, and in awe of their own incredible journey.

In this plush bungalow-turned-studio, I continue to push the boundaries of boudoir photography, forever captivated by the beauty and strength it uncovers. It's a place where art and passion merge, where stories are told through images, and where the human spirit is celebrated in all its raw, unapologetic glory.

I glance at my phone, a familiar buzz indicating the arrival of a new query. It's become a pre-requisite for me before taking on any project—a glimpse into the woman's world, her desires, and her expectations. And there it is, a message accompanied by three intriguing photos.

With eager anticipation, I open the message, ready to immerse myself in the visual journey that awaits. Each photograph tells a story—a story of vulnerability, strength, and unspoken desires. As my eyes scan the images, I become captivated by the nuances captured within each frame.

In the first photo, she stands tall wearing a black flowy gown, her eyes gazing into the distance with an air of confidence. Her body language exudes a quiet power, a determination to embrace her true self. It's a portrait that speaks volumes—a declaration of her journey towards self-love and acceptance.

The second photo reveals a different side—a moment of vulnerability and intimacy. Her gaze is averted, a hint of shyness painting her features. Soft tendrils of hair cascade down her shoulders, adding an ethereal touch to the composition. In this frame, I sense a desire to be seen, to be cherished for the unique beauty that resides within.

The third photo, a playful capture, exudes vibrant energy. She laughs, unabashedly embracing joy and freedom. The light dances upon her face, casting a warm glow that mirrors the fire within. It's a snapshot of pure bliss—a celebration of life and the uninhibited spirit that resides within us all.

As I study each photograph, I begin to understand her on a deeper level. Her hopes, her dreams, her fears—they all unfold before me, etched into the pixels of these images. It's a privilege to be granted this glimpse into her world, to bear witness to the essence of her being.

These photographs serve as a bridge—a connection between her story and my artistry. They provide the foundation upon which I can craft an experience that will surpass her expectations, capturing the very essence of who she is. They guide me, fuelling my imagination as I envision the possibilities that lie ahead.

With each new query, each set of photographs, I am reminded of the trust bestowed upon me. It's not just about taking pictures—it's about creating an experience, an opportunity for self-discovery and empowerment. These images are more than mere visuals; they are windows into the soul—a glimpse into the depths of human emotion.

Looking at the photos, I just knew I had to take it.

So, with these photographs as my guide, I prepare to embark on a journey. A journey that will intertwine her desires and my artistry, creating an exquisite tapestry of boudoir photography. As I type out my response, I carry her hopes and expectations in my heart, ready to transform her vision into a tangible reality—a celebration of her unique beauty, captured through the lens of my camera.

***

Chapter 3 – Unleashing My Sensuality
Nivedita's POV

Sahil has agreed to do the boudoir; I knew he would not say no. Now, I have to prepare for the photoshoot. Ajay, my fiancé, doesn't know about my little adventure.

He doesn't have to.

With a surge of excitement, I read Sahil's response—my favourite boudoir photographer has agreed to capture my essence through his lens. I knew he wouldn't say no. Now, it's time to embark on the journey of preparation, to ensure that every detail is in place for the upcoming photoshoot.

First things first, I dive into researching the perfect boudoir wardrobe. I spend hours scouring boutiques and online stores, seeking out lingerie pieces that will reflect my personality and make me feel like a goddess. It's not just about looking good; it's about feeling confident and comfortable in my own skin. From delicate lace to daring corsets, I curate a collection that captures the different facets of my femininity.

As I embark on the exhilarating journey of preparing for the boudoir photoshoot, I find myself immersed in a world of shopping—a delightful quest to find the perfect pieces that embody the bridal theme while exuding sensuality and sophistication.

I begin my shopping escapade by exploring bridal boutiques, enchanted by racks adorned with exquisite lace, delicate embroidery, and whispers of tulle. I try on a myriad of lingerie sets, searching for the ones that will evoke the essence of a blushing bride while igniting a fire within. Each piece is carefully chosen, with attention to detail—romantic bralettes adorned with intricate floral patterns, satin garters delicately trimmed with lace, and ethereal robes that cascade effortlessly around the contours of my body.

Embracing the bridal theme, I also delve into the world of white lingerie—creamy satin, whisper-soft chiffon, and intricately embellished corsets that sculpt and accentuate my curves. I aim for a balance between elegance and allure, selecting pieces that allow me to feel both angelic and fiercely seductive. It's a dance of contrasts, a celebration of femininity and empowerment.

In my quest for variety, I also explore the world of lingerie in hues that complement my skin tone and evoke a sense of romance. Delicate blush pinks, sultry burgundies, and daring blacks find their way into my shopping bag, adding a touch of mystery and intrigue to the collection. Every piece serves a purpose—to captivate, to tell a story, and to leave an indelible impression.

Accessories become an essential part of the ensemble, amplifying the allure and elevating the bridal theme. I seek out dainty pearl necklaces that grace my collarbones, delicate lace gloves that encase my hands with elegance, and whimsical floral headpieces that crown me with a touch of ethereal beauty. Each accessory is carefully selected to enhance the narrative, adding a layer of sophistication and whimsy to the visual tale.

As I shop, I keep in mind the transformative nature of boudoir photography—a chance to shed inhibitions and embrace vulnerability. I choose fabrics that caress the skin, allowing for freedom of movement, while still exuding an air of elegance and grace. Comfort is paramount, as it creates the space for me to fully immerse myself in the experience, confident in the knowledge that every piece has been thoughtfully chosen to enhance my beauty and showcase my individuality.

With each shopping excursion, I relish the anticipation of unveiling these meticulously selected treasures to Sahil. I imagine the look on his face as he sees the pieces come together, the sparkle in his eyes as he envisions the artistry that will unfold during our photoshoot.

As I step out of the boutiques, bags filled with carefully curated lingerie, accessories, and delicate garments, I am filled with a sense of excitement and wonder. These pieces hold the promise of transformation—a journey that will unfold before the lens of the camera, capturing the essence of my bridal spirit, celebrating my sensuality, and ultimately creating art that will forever remind me of this extraordinary chapter in my life.

Next, I turn my attention to grooming. I want to feel pampered and radiant, so I book an appointment at a high-end salon for a luxurious spa treatment. As I indulge in the blissful moments of relaxation, I envision the images that Sahil will capture—the softness of my skin, the glow of my complexion—a canvas ready to be adorned with his artistry.

I also reach out to a talented hair and makeup artist, someone who can enhance my natural features while staying true to my personal style. Together, we experiment with different looks, playing with colours, textures, and techniques. I want the final result to be an exquisite blend of elegance and allure—a reflection of the woman I have become.

In the days leading up to the photo shoot, I focus on nourishing my body and mind. I incorporate healthy habits into my routine—nutritious meals, rejuvenating workouts, and moments of mindfulness. It's important for me to feel strong and centred, to radiate positive energy that will shine through in the photographs.

I also take the time to curate a playlist—a collection of songs that resonate with my journey, that evoke the emotions I want to channel during the photoshoot. The right music has the power to transport me, to bring out my inner goddess, and I want every moment of the experience to be accompanied by a melody that sets the perfect tone.

As the day of the photoshoot draws near, a mix of excitement and nervous anticipation fills my being. I remind myself that this is a celebration—an opportunity to embrace my sensuality, to honour my body, and to capture a moment in time that I will cherish forever.

I trust in Sahil's vision and expertise, knowing that he will guide me through the process with care and sensitivity. Together, we will create art—images that tell a story, that capture the essence of who I am in this moment. And when I look back on these photographs, I know they will serve as a reminder of my strength, my beauty, and my journey towards self-love.

So, with the preparations complete and my heart brimming with excitement, I eagerly await the day when Sahil and I will come together, merging our creative energies to weave a tale of empowerment and beauty. The countdown begins, and I can't help but feel a sense of anticipation building—an anticipation for the transformation that awaits, for the magic that will unfold in the presence of the camera.

I am readying for my first boudoir photography, and I'm excited,

A moment to embrace my beauty, where inhibitions are ignited.

In the tender folds of lace and silk, I'll unveil my allure,

Capturing my essence, a celebration of self I will ensure.

As the soft light caresses my skin, a canvas for desire,

I step into a realm where confidence soars higher.

In this intimate dance, I am the muse, the embodiment of grace,

Exploring my sensuality with a smile on my face.

With each delicate pose, I'll unveil layers unseen,

A tapestry of passion, where vulnerability gleams.

I'll adorn myself with confidence, like jewels on display,

Embracing my curves, as art in its most elegant array.

My body, a symphony of lines, curves, and whispers,

A testament to resilience, strength, and inner blizzards.

For this is not just a photograph, but a love letter to me,

A celebration of my journey, the woman I've come to be.

In front of the lens, I'll shed societal expectations,

Embracing my authenticity, without hesitations.

No longer confined by judgment's heavy shroud,

I'll emerge as a masterpiece, fierce and unbowed.

For this moment is mine, a chapter of liberation,

A chance to honour my spirit with unwavering dedication.

I'll radiate confidence, like a flame that never dies,

Revelling in the truth that beauty truly resides.

So, as I embark on this journey, a dance of vulnerability and pride,

I'll savour the anticipation, with passion as my guide.

For boudoir photography is more than mere art,

It's an affirmation of self, a journey to my heart.

Chapter 4 – A Captivating Encounter

Sahil's POV

I step into my studio, the familiar scent of creativity and anticipation filling the air. As I enter the space that has witnessed countless stories unfold, my eyes meet a sight that leaves me breathless. Standing before me is an ethereal vision, a woman whose beauty surpasses any description I could conjure. She's undoubtedly the most gorgeous woman I have ever met.

Her presence commands attention, radiating a confidence that dances with a touch of vulnerability. Her eyes, like pools of liquid gold, shimmer with a fire that sets my heart ablaze. Her smile, a captivating curve that ignites a spark within me, reveals a glimpse of the vibrant spirit that resides within me. It's as if the very essence of boudoir photography has taken human form before my eyes.

My fingers instinctively reach for my camera, eager to capture this moment—her presence, her aura, her story. I find myself mesmerized by the way the light caresses her flawless complexion, highlighting the delicate curve of her cheekbones and the gentle sweep of her jawline. It's as if she was sculpted by the gods themselves, an exquisite masterpiece waiting to be immortalized through my lens.

As I approach her, a wave of excitement and nervous anticipation washes over me. I am keenly aware of the responsibility I hold—to capture her essence, her unique beauty, in a way that transcends the ordinary. This is a collaboration, a dance between two artists—one behind the camera, the other in front—each contributing their own energy to create something extraordinary.

"Hey, I'm Nivedita," she says with a smile.

It was the first time I had to remind myself of my first rule: Never be aroused while doing the shoot.

Don't get me wrong. I'm not a robot. It's just that I take my work very seriously. Also, I have had my fair share with the fairer gender, and I have never felt that way while doing a shoot.

In the realm of boudoir photography, my journey has been a vibrant tapestry woven with diverse experiences and encounters.

It's a world where passion and artistry collide, where vulnerability and empowerment intertwine. And yes, it's true that throughout my career, I've been fortunate enough to cross paths with captivating women who exude charm and beauty.

But let me assure you, my dear reader, that the colourful tapestry of my life isn't about indulgence or excess. It's about navigating the delicate dance of connection and professionalism with grace and respect.

Each woman who steps into my studio brings with her a unique story—a story that deserves to be cherished, honoured, and captured through the lens of my camera. From the hesitant brides-to-be seeking to embrace their sensuality to the confident souls basking in the fullness of their femininity, each encounter is an opportunity to celebrate the diverse expressions of womanhood.

While it's true that there have been moments when admiration has been expressed, I have always approached these situations with a firm understanding of my role as a photographer. I recognize the importance of boundaries and the necessity of maintaining professionalism throughout every interaction.

A key aspect of my success lies in building trust and fostering an environment where women can feel safe, supported, and empowered. The connection we forge during a boudoir session is not based on superficiality or fleeting desires; it is born out of a mutual understanding and respect for the vulnerability that is shared.

I take pride in being able to create a space where women feel comfortable expressing their true selves—where they can shed societal expectations and explore their desires, fears, and dreams. It is within this space that the true magic of boudoir photography unfolds—a transformation that transcends the physical and touches the very essence of their being.

While my experiences may have been colourful, they have always been approached with sensitivity and an unwavering commitment to the art form. I am humbled by the trust these women place in me and the opportunity to capture their unique beauty.

Through my lens, I strive to create images that celebrate their individuality, ignite their confidence, and serve as a reminder of their strength and worth.

So, in my journey through the vibrant landscape of boudoir photography, know that my focus remains on artistry, the connection, and the celebration of the human spirit. It's a world where sensuality and empowerment coexist—a world where the colours of life come alive in the most tasteful and meaningful way.

But I couldn't take my eyes off Nivedita.

"Come in, let's have a seat and discuss what you want from this session," I say, finally finding my voice.

Chapter 5 – Capturing My Essence

Nivedita's POV

I sit across from Sahil, excitement bubbling within me as I prepare to share my vision for the boudoir photoshoot. The studio is filled with a sense of anticipation, and I can't help but feel a wave of gratitude for having such a talented photographer to guide me through this transformative experience.

"Sahil," I begin, leaning forward, "I have some ideas in mind for the shoot, but I'm also open to your expert input. I want these photos to capture not only my sensuality but also my personality—a true reflection of who I am as a woman."

Sahil listens attentively, his gaze focused, as I delve into my desires. I share my love for vibrant colours and the way they evoke joy and playfulness within me. I express my desire to incorporate elements that represent my passions—a book that symbolizes my love for literature, and a bouquet of wildflowers that speaks to my free-spirited nature.

He nods thoughtfully, taking mental notes.

"I love your ideas, Nivedita," Sahil responds, his voice brimming with enthusiasm. "Incorporating personal elements into the shoot is a wonderful way to infuse the images with your unique essence. It adds depth and authenticity."

We dive into a collaborative brainstorming session, bouncing ideas back and forth. Sahil's suggestions are invaluable, as he offers insights into lighting techniques, poses, and framing that can best showcase my personality and desired mood. He shares his expertise in capturing the interplay between shadows and highlights, and how they can add depth and mystery to the images. It's evident that he not only possesses technical mastery but also a keen eye for storytelling.

Together, we craft a plan—a visual narrative that intertwines sensuality, self-expression, and a touch of whimsy. Sahil's suggestions align seamlessly with my vision, enhancing it and bringing it to life in ways I couldn't have imagined.

As we finalize the details, I feel an overwhelming sense of trust in Sahil's ability to capture the essence of who I am. His passion for his craft shines through in every word he speaks, instilling confidence and excitement for the upcoming photoshoot.

Before parting ways, we discuss wardrobe choices and the significance they can hold in telling my story. Sahil advises me on selecting pieces that not only flatter my figure but also resonate with my desired aesthetic. We discuss the interplay between textures, colours, and fabrics, aiming to create a harmonious visual tapestry that reflects my inner world.

As I leave the studio that day, a sense of anticipation washes over me. I'm filled with gratitude for having found a photographer who not only understands my vision but also possesses the skill to bring it to life. The collaborative process has solidified my trust in Sahil's artistic prowess and his commitment to capturing the true essence of who I am.

In the days leading up to the shoot, I find myself eagerly preparing, gathering the wardrobe pieces that will be an extension of my personality. Sahil's guidance echoes in my mind as I carefully select garments that embody my desired mood and showcase my individuality.

With each passing day, the excitement builds, knowing that I am about to embark on a transformative journey—one that will celebrate my sensuality, capture my personality, and create a collection of images that will forever hold a special place in my heart.

As I eagerly anticipate the day of the shoot, I am filled with gratitude for the collaborative partnership I have found in Sahil. Together, we are embarking on a creative adventure—a shared vision to create art that not only celebrates my journey but also inspires and empowers others to embrace their true selves.

And so, with a heart brimming with anticipation, I prepare to step into the world of boudoir photography—a world where vulnerability meets empowerment, and where the essence of who I am will be beautifully captured through the lens of Sahil's artistry.

Chapter 6 – The Boudoir Shoot

Sahil's POV

Day 1:

I step into my meticulously designed studio, a surge of anticipation coursing through my veins. Today, I am about to embark on a new boudoir journey—a dance of art and intimacy that will unfold before the lens of my camera. As I prepare the lighting and adjust the props, I can't help but feel a hint of excitement tinged with a touch of nervousness.

Ah, it's time to capture Nivedita's grace and sensuality.

It's not every day that I photograph a boudoir session with a bride-to-be. The air is thick with a sense of reverence and celebration—a unique blend of vulnerability and empowerment. I remind myself of my first rule, the one I've held close since the beginning—never be aroused while doing the shoot. It's not because I'm a cold-hearted robot, but rather because I take my work incredibly seriously. There's a sacredness to capturing these moments, and maintaining a professional demeanour allows me to honour the trust and vulnerability of my clients.

As Nivedita walks through the studio doors, radiating an ethereal beauty, my breath catches in my throat. She embodies the essence of a blushing bride—her eyes sparkling with anticipation, her movements graceful yet confident. I can't deny the electric energy that crackles between us, the natural chemistry that arises in such intimate settings. But I quickly push those thoughts aside, refocusing on my role as the artist capturing her journey.

We exchange pleasantries, and I guide Nivedita through the studio, pointing out the different sets and backdrops we can use. Together, we create an atmosphere of trust and camaraderie—a safe space where she can fully embrace her sensuality and vulnerability.

As we begin the photo shoot, I meticulously frame each shot, ensuring that the composition captures her essence. I offer gentle guidance, suggesting poses that accentuate her best features and convey the desired emotions. It's a delicate balance between directing and allowing her to express her unique personality—an intricate dance of collaboration.

Nivedita blossoms before my lens, embracing her femininity with newfound confidence. She effortlessly transitions between sultry gazes, playful laughter, and moments of quiet introspection. Each click of the camera captures a fleeting expression, a glimpse into the depths of her soul.

I find myself marvelling at the artistry of the human form—the subtle curves, the play of light and shadow, and the raw emotions that radiate from within. It's a privilege to witness the transformation that unfolds during a boudoir shoot—to be granted access to the innermost layers of a person's being.

As I click away, my focus remains unwavering. I immerse myself in the technical aspects—the lighting, the composition, the framing. It's a form of discipline, an anchor that keeps me grounded amidst the charged atmosphere. I remind myself of the trust that Nivedita has placed in me, the responsibility I hold to honour her vulnerability.

During the shoot, I draw upon my experience and intuition, seamlessly blending the art of photography with the art of connection. I create a space where Nivedita feels supported, celebrated, and empowered. I offer words of encouragement, affirming her beauty and the strength she exudes. It's not just about capturing stunning images—it's about fostering an environment where she can explore her desires, embrace her authenticity, and celebrate her journey.

As the session draws to a close, I take a moment to reflect on the transformative power of boudoir photography. It's not just about the captivating images that will grace the final album—it's about the profound impact it has on the individuals involved. I've witnessed tears of joy, moments of self-discovery, and the quiet triumph of self-acceptance.

With a sense of accomplishment, I wrap up the shoot. Nivedita's radiant smile and the sparkle in her eyes serves as a testament to the experience we've shared—a testament to the magic that can be created when artistry and vulnerability intertwine.

As I bid Nivedita farewell, I can't help but feel a tinge of nostalgia. Each boudoir session is a fleeting moment—a chapter in someone's story. And as I review the photographs, selecting the ones that truly capture the essence of Nivedita's journey, I am reminded once again of the privilege and responsibility I hold as a boudoir photographer.

In the quiet of my studio, surrounded by the remnants of our creative collaboration, I take a moment to appreciate the intricacies of my craft. Boudoir photography is more than just capturing sensual moments—it's about honouring vulnerability, celebrating individuality, and creating art that empowers and inspires.

With renewed passion and a sense of purpose, I set to work, pouring over the images, and carefully selecting the ones that encapsulate the spirit of Nivedita's bridal boudoir. Each photograph tells a story, a testament to her strength, her beauty, and her journey towards self-love. And as I prepare the final collection, I can't help but feel a profound sense of gratitude—for the trust placed in me, for the opportunity to be a part of these intimate narratives, and for the privilege of being a witness to the transformative power of boudoir photography.

Day 2:

As I enter the exquisitely designed boudoir set, my breath catches in my throat at the sight of Nivedita. Bathed in the soft glow of the carefully placed lighting, she stands in the centre of the lounge, adorned in delicate lace lingerie that embraces her curves with sheer elegance. Every detail, from the intricate patterns to the way the fabric drapes gently against her skin, speaks of sensuality and sophistication.

With each click of the shutter, I capture the subtle nuances of her pose—the way her hand delicately grazes her collarbone, and the slight tilt of her head that exudes a captivating confidence. Her eyes, filled with a mix of vulnerability and empowerment, meet mine, and for a moment, time stands still. In that instant, I am reminded of the privilege bestowed upon me—the privilege of capturing the essence of a woman embracing her sensuality.

The ambient music playing softly in the background sets the mood, adding a touch of enchantment to the scene. As Nivedita moves gracefully, the natural curves of her body create mesmerizing lines and shadows, inviting my lens to capture the interplay of light and form. The textures of the surrounding furnishings—the plush velvet chaise lounge, and the vintage mirrored vanity—provide a backdrop that complements her beauty, enhancing the overall aesthetic.

I guide Nivedita with gentle suggestions, encouraging her to explore different poses that showcase her unique allure. She gracefully transitions from standing to reclining on the chaise lounge, her body language radiating both vulnerability and strength. With each pose, I aim to capture the essence of her femininity—the curve of her hips, the arch of her back, and the delicate playfulness of her expression.

The atmosphere in the room is electric, charged with creative energy and mutual trust. I strive to create an environment where Nivedita feels not only comfortable but also empowered—a space where she can fully embrace her sensuality without reservation. It is within these moments that the true magic of boudoir photography unfolds—a celebration of self-love, body positivity, and the art of capturing the beauty that resides within.

Throughout the shoot, I experiment with different angles and perspectives, capturing close-ups that highlight the intricate details of the lace against her skin and wide shots that encompass the entire scene, framing her in a tableau of sensuous beauty. Every image is carefully composed, seeking to evoke emotion, ignite desire, and tell a story—a story of a woman embracing her authenticity and celebrating her journey.

As the session draws to a close, I know that we have created something extraordinary—a collection of images that encapsulates the essence of Nivedita's sensuality, her confidence, and her journey of self-discovery. The artistic boudoir we have crafted together transcends the realm of mere photography—it becomes a testament to the power of embracing one's desires and finding empowerment in vulnerability.

With a sense of fulfilment, I lower my camera and meet Nivedita's gaze. There is a shared understanding, a silent acknowledgement of the profound experience we have just shared. The memories captured in these images will forever serve as a reminder of her beauty, her strength, and her journey of self-acceptance—a celebration of the woman she is and the woman she is becoming.

In that intimate moment, I feel a profound sense of gratitude—for the trust she placed in me, for the opportunity to witness her transformation, and for the privilege of creating art that celebrates the beauty and sensuality that resides within each and every one of us.

Day 3:

Nivedita was sitting on the couch, with her back to the camera and her back arched.

I adjust the lighting in the studio, casting a soft, warm glow that caresses every curve and contour of the room. The atmosphere is charged with anticipation as Nivedita takes her position on the plush couch, her back gracefully arched, and her silhouette bathed in the gentle illumination.

With a steady hand, I raise the camera to my eye, my focus honed on capturing the essence of this intimate moment. The click of the shutter resonates through the air, freezing time as I immortalize the sensuality that radiates from Nivedita's pose.

From behind the lens, I admire the curves of her back, the elegant arch that accentuates her feminine form. The soft fabric of her lingerie traces delicate lines against her skin, teasing the eye and leaving much to the imagination. It's a moment of vulnerability and empowerment—a celebration of her unique beauty.

As I continue to capture the essence of this artistic boudoir session, I experiment with different angles and perspectives. I move around the room, exploring how the interplay of light and shadow can enhance the composition. Each click of the shutter paints a portrait of seduction and self-assurance—a testament to the power of the human form.

The artistry of the moment lies not only in Nivedita's alluring pose but also in the subtle details that surround her. The carefully selected props—a cascade of rose petals tumbling from a nearby table, a vintage book resting beside her—add depth and layers of symbolism to the scene. They become supporting characters in this visual narrative, inviting the viewer to engage with their own imagination and interpretation.

As the shoot progresses, I encourage Nivedita to explore different expressions, inviting her to reveal facets of her personality that go beyond the physical. Her laughter, her subtle smoulder, and the quiet vulnerability in her eyes—each moment encapsulates a part of her story, a glimpse into her soul.

With each frame, I strive to capture the intimacy and connection between Nivedita and the camera—a connection that transcends the physical and delves into the depths of her being. It's a dance between subject and artist, a collaboration where trust and creativity intertwine.

Throughout the session, I am keenly aware of the delicate balance between capturing the sensuality of the moment and maintaining the utmost respect for Nivedita's boundaries. It's an art form that requires finesse and sensitivity, and I hold myself to the highest standards of professionalism.

As I review the images later, I am captivated by the raw beauty that unfolds before me. The arch of her back, the play of light on her skin, and the subtle curve of her lips—all harmonize to create a visual symphony of sensuality and artistry.

In these photographs, I have not only captured a moment in time but also immortalized a journey of self-discovery and empowerment. Each image tells a story—a story of vulnerability, strength, and the celebration of womanhood.

As I set the camera aside, I feel a profound sense of gratitude—for the trust Nivedita placed in me, for the opportunity to capture her essence, and for being a witness to the transformative power of boudoir photography. In these moments, I am reminded once again why I fell in love with this art form—because within its confines, beauty, intimacy, and self-expression converge in the most extraordinary way.

Day 4:

As I enter the exquisitely designed boudoir set, a sense of anticipation fills the air. The room is bathed in soft, diffused light, casting a gentle glow upon Nivedita's radiant form as she reclines on the plush bed. Every detail has been meticulously arranged to create an atmosphere of sensuality and elegance.

With each click of my camera, I capture intimate moments that transcend the physical, weaving a tapestry of emotions and desires. I approach the shoot with reverence, embracing the delicate dance between vulnerability and empowerment.

Nivedita's eyes meet mine, brimming with a mixture of confidence and anticipation. Her tousled hair cascades gently upon the pillow, framing her face like a halo. I focus on capturing the essence of her beauty, the delicate lines and contours that make her unique.

As she shifts, her body language speaks volumes—a subtle invitation, a hint of vulnerability. I guide her with gentle suggestions, capturing moments that exude both grace and passion. The curve of her hip, the arch of her back, each pose crafted with artistic intention, celebrating her femininity.

I observe the interplay of shadows and light, allowing them to caress her skin with a painterly touch. The soft fabric of her lingerie creates a sensual contrast against the delicate curves of her body. I capture the textures—the lace, the silk—as they accentuate her allure, capturing the essence of both vulnerability and strength.

Nivedita's gaze meets the camera with a mix of confidence and vulnerability, her eyes reflecting a myriad of emotions. In each photograph, I strive to encapsulate the complexity of her journey—the triumphs, the vulnerabilities, and the moments of self-discovery.

The atmosphere in the room is charged with intangible energy—a palpable connection between photographer and subject, artist and muse. As I compose each shot, I am keenly aware of the trust Nivedita has placed in me, and I honour it with every click of the shutter.

Through the lens, I capture the subtle details—the play of light upon her skin, the rise and fall of her breath, the delicate curve of her lips, the tempting swell of her breasts. Each image tells a story—a narrative of beauty, desire, and self-acceptance.

In the midst of the shoot, there is a moment—an intimate pause where time seems to stand still. Nivedita's vulnerability is laid bare, her authentic self-shining through. It is in these raw and unguarded moments that the true power of boudoir photography reveals itself—a celebration of self-love, an affirmation of beauty in all its forms.

As the shoot comes to a close, I review the images with a mixture of satisfaction and awe. The artistry, the sensuality, and the depth captured within each frame leave me breathless. This boudoir session with Nivedita has been a testament to the beauty and power that can be found in embracing one's true self.

I feel a sense of gratitude for the trust Nivedita has bestowed upon me—to be a witness to her journey, to capture her essence in a collection of photographs that will forever hold her story.

As I pack up my equipment, a sense of fulfilment washes over me. This boudoir session has been a culmination of artistry, vulnerability, and the celebration of feminine empowerment. I am reminded once again why I am drawn to this extraordinary world of boudoir photography—a world where intimacy meets art, and where beauty is captured in its most authentic and alluring form.

Chapter 7 - A Tense Conversation

Nivedita's POV

As I step into the realm of intimacy's grace,

I weave my desires with elegance, in this sacred space.

In the soft hues of candlelight, secrets start to bloom,

A conversation of vulnerability in this boudoir's room.

Gently I share my wishes, with confidence and poise,

As I unveil the fantasies that my heart truly enjoys.

With every whispered word, I paint a passionate scene,

Where my desires, like silk, cascade in a seductive sheen.

A moment frozen in time, as trust intertwines,

In this haven of sensuality, where pleasure defines.

I reveal my longing, my yearning, my dreams,

Each delicate detail, as radiant as moonlit streams.

In the gentle strokes of light, the camera's gentle hum,

I surrender to the moment, feeling blissfully undone.

No judgment or restraint, just freedom to explore,

To let my inner fire burn, like never before.

The lens captures my essence, my fierce sensuous grace,

Unveiling my vulnerability with an artistry's embrace.

In this dance of vulnerability, I find strength anew,

A celebration of my body, as it is, pure and true.

With each click of the shutter, a moment unfolds,

An intimate narrative, intricately told.

This boudoir session, a journey of self-discovery,

A tapestry of desires woven, with my consent as the key.

As the session concludes, I stand tall and free,

The empowerment of self-love, a radiant decree.

For in the boudoir's embrace, I found my inner light,

A celebration of my sensuality, a soul ignited, taking flight.

So let the photographs speak a thousand tales,

Of a woman reclaiming her desires, without veils.

For in this boudoir session, I unveiled my truth,

A testament to self-acceptance, forever in youth.

We have just finished the shoot. It has been the most liberating experience of my life. In the past four days, I have realized what makes Sahil such a great photographer. He understands me as much as I understand myself. He's so professional when it comes to work.

And yet, I sense an underlying tension between us.

Sexual tension!

My phone rings, and as I glance at the caller ID, my heart sinks. It's Ajay, mu fiancé.

"Excuse me!" I tell Sahil and step away. Taking a deep breath, I answer the call, already bracing myself for what is to come.

"Hey, Ajay," I say, trying to keep my voice steady.

"What the hell is this, Nivedita?" His voice cuts through the line, filled with anger and disappointment. "I just found out about this boudoir shoot you're doing. Are you out of your mind?"

I can feel the tension building, the weight of his disapproval pressing down on me.

"Ajay, I didn't expect you to react this way. It's something I wanted to do for myself, to embrace my sensuality and feel empowered."

He scoffs, his voice dripping with disdain.

"Empowered? More like degrading yourself for attention. Do you think this is what a respectable woman does? It's nothing but sleazy and cheap."

His words sting, hitting me with a force I hadn't anticipated. I take a moment to steady myself, my voice trembling slightly.

"Ajay, this is about me reclaiming my confidence, embracing my body, and celebrating my journey. It's not about seeking attention or degrading myself."

He lets out a bitter laugh.

"Well, it certainly seems like you're seeking attention. What's next, Nivedita? Are you going to parade yourself half-naked for the world to see? Have you no self-respect?" his voice breaks as he shrieks.

His hurtful words pierce through me, and tears threaten to spill from my eyes. I gather my strength, refusing to let his judgment erode my self-worth. "Ajay, this is a personal choice, and I would appreciate it if you could try to understand and support me, even if you don't agree with it."

"Oh, I understand perfectly," he retorts, his voice dripping with sarcasm. "You're more interested in your own desires and fantasies than in our relationship. I thought I knew who you were, Nivedita, but now I'm not so sure."

His accusation hits me like a dagger to the heart. I never expected our conversation to take such a toxic turn.

"Ajay, this doesn't change who I am as a person or what I feel for you. It's about embracing my individuality, and I hope you can find it in yourself to respect that," I say. Even though I'm trying not to get emotional, tears sting my eyes.

Damn you, Ajay!

"Respect? You want me to respect this nonsense?" he scoffs. "I can't respect someone who devalues themselves in such a way. I thought I had a partner who had integrity and self-respect, but I guess I was wrong."

The tears finally spill over, sliding down my cheeks as his words cut deep. I gather my strength, my voice laced with a mix of sadness and determination.

"If you can't accept me for who I am and support me in my journey of self-discovery, then maybe we need to re-evaluate our relationship."

There's a moment of silence on the other end of the line, and I can almost feel the weight of his realization. But before I can utter another word, he hangs up abruptly, leaving me with a mix of emotions—heartache, anger, and a newfound resolve to embrace my own path, regardless of the obstacles.

"Let's call it off. You can live your own life of voyeur. I can't," he says.

Before I can say a word, he hangs up.

Oh, well!

As I wipe away my tears, I take a deep breath, reminding myself that I am deserving of love, respect, and the freedom to explore and express myself. The hurtful words of Ajay linger, but they will not define me. I am stronger than the judgments of others, and I will continue to pursue my own happiness and empowerment, even if it means making difficult choices along the way.

With renewed determination, I gather my courage, ready to face the challenges that lie ahead. This boudoir shoot is not just about capturing beautiful images—it's about reclaiming my voice, my confidence, and ultimately, my own happiness.

As my heart aches and tears stain my face,

I stand here wounded, caught in love's embrace.

My dearest love, why must you turn away,

For a boudoir session, where my spirit found sway?

In the depths of my being, I sought to reclaim,

The voice that once whispered, longing for no shame.

A boudoir, a celebration of my strength and grace,

A testament to the beauty within this fragile space.

But you, my love, questioned my intentions pure,

Unable to see the essence of my allure.

In vulnerability, I sought to rediscover,

The confidence within, my own soul's lover.

I stand here now, shattered, yet resolute,

To reclaim my voice, to find my truth.

For happiness resides within my own embrace,

No longer bound by your judgments, I'll find my own space.

With each passing day, I'll mend my broken heart,

Nurturing the fragments, reclaiming every part.

For self-love knows no boundaries or control,

It blooms within me, a flame that won't be doused or stole.

I'll find solace in the whispers of the wind,

Embracing my sensuality, unapologetically thinned.

In boudoir's embrace, I'll cherish my essence,

A reminder of my strength, a testament to resilience.

Though your absence stings, I'll forge my way,

For my happiness is not defined by your stay.

I'll rise from the ashes, reborn and renewed,

With confidence ablaze, my spirit will exude.

So, my love, as you bid our love farewell,

Know that I'll reclaim my voice, my story to tell.

In the boudoir's shadows, I'll find my light,

And rediscover the joy that ignites my inner sight.

For the journey ahead, though uncertain it seems,
I'll bask in my own radiance, pursue my dreams.
With newfound confidence, I'll dance on my own,
Revelling in my happiness, to myself, I'll be known.

So, farewell, my love, with gratitude I part,
For through this pain, I'll reclaim my heart.
In the pursuit of my happiness, I'll find my way,
And celebrate the woman I am, every single day.

Chapter 8 – Tension in the Air

Sahil's POV

I observe Nivedita as she engages in a phone conversation, her face tense and filled with worry. Yet, even in the midst of her inner turmoil, her beauty remains an enchanting sight.

We are still in the bedroom, embraced by the serene beauty. Outside, the sun has begun its descent, casting a golden hue across the sky as if paying homage to Nivedita's ethereal presence. Her countenance, marked by delicate furrows on her brow, reveals the weight of her concerns. But it is her physical allure that captivates me, despite the tension she carries.

Nivedita's cascading locks, the color of rich ebony, flow like a graceful river, swaying gently with the touch of the breeze. They dance in harmony with the surroundings, as if nature itself recognizes the poetic beauty that resides within her. The soft rays of twilight caress her flawless skin, highlighting its porcelain complexion and accentuating the grace that emanates from deep within.

Her eyes, shimmering like stars in the night sky, hold a myriad of stories untold. They mirror both resilience and strength, refusing to yield in the face of her burdens. While her worries may cloud her mind, her spirit remains unyielding, casting a glow that surpasses any shadow that may attempt to dim her radiance.

With a sigh, Nivedita concludes her phone call. Yet, even in that moment, a gentle smile graces her lips, revealing a glimmer of hope amidst the turmoil. It is a testament to her unwavering spirit, a flicker of optimism that persists despite the challenges she faces.

The scene surrounding us adds to the tranquil ambiance. The bedroom, bathed in the soft glow of twilight, stretch into the distance. Majestic mountains stand sentinel against the horizon, their presence a silent witness to Nivedita's inner strength.

Moved by her elegance and the turmoil she carries, I step closer to her. A surge of tenderness fills my heart, a yearning to alleviate her worries and bring her joy. In her eyes, I glimpse a universe of grace, a longing to shield her from the world's hardships and hold her in a comforting embrace.

"Is everything okay?"

Her response is a simple.

"Yeah!" Yet, there's a hint of something hiding beneath the surface, a veil of unease that lingers.

"Was that your fiancé?" I probe, hoping to understand the source of her hidden distress.

"Yeah," she replies, but her smile fails to reach her eyes. There's a subtle melancholy, a weight in her voice that tugs at my heart.

In that moment, I realize there's more to the story, a deeper narrative that yearns to be unveiled. As Sahil, her fiancé, I can't help but feel a pang of concern and curiosity, sensing that something important is amiss.

She doesn't want to discuss, perhaps, so I don't probe her much. For now, I remain by her side, a steadfast companion in the face of her struggles. As the twilight deepens and stars begin to dot the sky, I vow to be her support and pillar of strength. Together, we shall navigate the challenges that lie ahead, finding solace and respite in each other's company.

Nivedita, a woman of captivating spirit and undeniable beauty, deserves to be cherished. In her presence, I am reminded of the delicate balance between vulnerability and strength, and I am honoured to witness her journey towards reclaiming her voice, confidence, and ultimate happiness.

Chapter 9 – Unveiling Shadows

Sahil's POV

Nivedita's voice trembles slightly as she confirms that it was indeed her fiancé on the other end of the call. I can sense the tension radiating from her, a heaviness that lingers in the air between us.

"You don't look okay. Are you sure everything is okay?" I inquire gently, my concern evident in my tone.

"Yeah," Nivedita replies, her response accompanied by a half-hearted smile that fails to reach her eyes. The lines of worry etched upon her face betray her true emotions, and it's clear that something deeper is troubling her.

I hesitate for a moment, contemplating whether to delve further into the matter. But my intuition nudges me to offer support, to create a safe space for her to express herself if she chooses to do so.

"I don't want to be intruding but what did your fiancé say?" I inquire, hoping that my genuine curiosity will encourage her to open up.

"He doesn't like me doing *this*," Nivedita reveals, her voice tinged with a mixture of sadness and resignation.

I pause, taking in her words and the complex emotions underlying them. I understand that her fiancé's desire to be involved may stem from a place of concern or a need for reassurance. But I also recognize that this deeply personal journey of self-discovery is Nivedita's alone—an exploration of her identity and empowerment that may not necessarily align with her partner's expectations.

A compassionate silence settles between us as I consider the weight of Nivedita's words. It is not my place to influence her decision or guide her personal relationships, but I can offer support and empathy in this moment of vulnerability.

"Nivedita," I say gently, "I believe that boudoir photography is a deeply personal and empowering experience. It's an opportunity for you to embrace your individuality and celebrate your journey. While it's important to consider your partner's feelings, it's equally crucial to prioritize your own needs and desires."

She sighs softly, her eyes briefly meeting mine before looking away.

"I know... I just... I want to do this for myself, but it's hard when there are conflicting expectations."

I nod, understanding the internal struggle she faces.

"Navigating the complexities of relationships can be challenging, especially when it comes to matters of personal expression. It may be helpful to have an open and honest conversation with your fiancé, sharing your intentions, desires, and the importance of this experience for your own growth."

Nivedita takes a moment to absorb my words, her expression a mix of contemplation and uncertainty. She knows that this is a decision she must ultimately make for herself, balancing her individuality with the dynamics of her relationship.

"Thank you, Sahil," she finally says, her voice laced with gratitude. "Your understanding and support mean a lot to me."

I offer her a reassuring smile, hoping to provide a glimmer of solace in the midst of her inner turmoil. "You're welcome, Nivedita. Remember that this journey is about embracing your true self and finding empowerment. Trust yourself, and everything else will fall into place."

I can sense a renewed determination within Nivedita. She is now armed with the tools to navigate the complexities of her relationship and assert her own needs, all while embracing the transformative power of the boudoir experience.

At that moment, I realize that boudoir photography is not just about capturing beautiful images—it is about unveiling the shadows within, embracing vulnerability, and discovering the strength to stand tall in one's truth. I am grateful to be a part of Nivedita's journey, supporting her as she steps into her own power and finds the courage to express herself authentically, both in front of my camera and in her life beyond.

"Could you show me some couple poses?" she suddenly asks.

As a professional and respectful photographer, I remind myself to maintain a boundary between personal desires and the professional environment. While I appreciate Nivedita's beauty and vulnerability during the photo shoot, it is crucial to separate those feelings from my role as her photographer.

With a composed demeanour, I continue to guide Nivedita through the poses, focusing on capturing her essence and ensuring her comfort throughout the session. The connection we establish is one of trust and artistic collaboration, allowing her to explore her own journey of self-discovery.

It is natural to be drawn to someone's beauty and charisma, but as a professional, it is my duty to create a safe and respectful space for all clients. My focus remains on creating stunning images that empower and celebrate each individual, without allowing personal desires to interfere with the professional nature of the shoot.

I remind myself that boudoir photography is a platform for self-expression, empowerment, and celebrating one's unique journey. It is not an opportunity for personal fantasies or pursuits. By maintaining professionalism, I can create an environment where clients like Nivedita feel comfortable and confident, allowing their true selves to shine through the lens.

As the photoshoot continues, I redirect my attention back to capturing the essence of Nivedita's strength and vulnerability, preserving those fleeting moments of empowerment in timeless images. After all, as a photographer, my true passion lies in creating art that inspires and empowers others, not in pursuing personal desires that may compromise the integrity of my work.

I was so attracted to her at that moment. I wish it was me she was doing the photoshoot with. I would envelop her frame the back and hold her like a prized possession.

"Sure!" I nod.

As Nivedita expresses her desire to explore couple poses for her boudoir session, she looks to me for guidance. With utmost respect and sensitivity, I offer suggestions that honour the boundaries of tastefulness, capturing the essence of intimacy and connection between her and her husband.

"We can begin with an embrace in tender affection," I begin. "One beautiful pose to consider is where you and your husband embrace each other in a tender and affectionate manner. Stand facing each other, allowing your bodies to gently press together. Wrap your arms around each other, feeling the warmth and closeness. Turn your faces towards one another, gazing into each other's eyes, expressing the depth of your love. This pose captures the pure essence of your connection, showcasing the tenderness that exists between you."

Without me knowing, my voice becomes thick with desire. Nivedita asks me with her deep eyes with such longing, I wished I could demonstrate the pose to her.

"What else?" she asks, her voice raspy as well.

Is she feeling the same thing that I'm feeling?

"We can also explore the whispered secrets," I add.

"Show me," she asks.

"Pardon me!"

She slowly walks to the center of the bedroom and looks at me. "Show me the whispered secrets," she commands.

I feel myself drawn to her. I walk to her in a haze.

"Let's explore a pose that portrays a sense of intimacy through whispered secrets," I say as I stand behind her. "You can lean against your husband, resting your head gently on his chest," I say. Nivedita instinctively follows my instruction. The moment her body touches mine, I feel instantly aroused, more than before. "As he cradles you, his hand can caress your back or run through your hair, creating a soothing and intimate ambiance," I whisper in hear ear. "Engage in a quiet conversation or share whispered moments, allowing your love and trust to shine through. This pose symbolizes the sanctuary you find in each other, where secrets are shared, and hearts are heard."

Nivedita looks up at me, her eyes dark and intense.

"Tell me more," she says so softly, I would have missed it if her face wasn't so close to mine.

I swallow hard. It is getting harder to be near her. I guide her to the couch and gently sit her down.

"We can also capture the beautiful bond between you and your husband by showcasing the unity in your hands. You can sit or stand facing each other, letting your hands delicately intertwine," I say. Our fingers are now laced together. "This simple yet powerful gesture represents the connection you share on both an emotional and physical level. As your hands become one, it highlights the strength and solidarity of your relationship. It's a pose that conveys trust, support, and the beautiful entwining of your lives." I press my palm to hers, silently conveying what I want.

She smiled seductively and squeezes my heart, making my arousal getting wild.

"Tell me more, Sahil," she demands.

"Adding a playful touch to your couple poses can bring an element of joy and light-heartedness. You and your husband can engage in a moment of playful tenderness," I say.

"Ahnnn?"

I can see the message in her eyes.

She wants me just as much as I want her.

"Perhaps a gentle tickle," I graze a finger on her smooth arm, she hisses in response "Or a flirtatious glance, or a shared laughter that captures the spontaneous moments of happiness you experience together," I say as I stare into her eyes. "This pose showcases the fun-loving side of your relationship, reminding you both of the playful bond you share alongside the deeper intimacy."

"Deeper intimacy…" Nivedita muttered, her breath fanning my skin, titillating me.

"And there is another pose that celebrates the shared intimacy between you and your husband," I say. I guide her towards the plush bed, and she lets me. "Find a comfortable spot where you can sit or lie together," I say as I gently lay her on the bed, slowly sliding my body next to hers. Nivedita turns to look at me, her beautiful body stretching on the bed.

"Allow our bodies to naturally intertwine, creating a relaxed and serene composition," she says in a raspy voice, moving closer to me. She presses her body to mine, and wraps her right leg around my waist. I suck in a deep breath. She is taking charge, and I don't mind it.

Not one bit.

"The focus should be on capturing the closeness we feel, the gentleness of our touch, and the tenderness in our gazes," she speaks as her arms snakes around my neck. "This pose highlights the deep connection we have, showcasing the beauty of our shared moments of vulnerability and closeness," she adds and gently tugs the corner of my t-shirt.

Oh, boy!

Chapter 10 – The Serendipity

Sahil's POV

In a serendipitous twist of fate, Nivedita and I find ourselves locked in an embrace, succumbing to a brief but powerful moment of vulnerability. As our eyes meet, undeniable chemistry filled the air, drawing us closer with each passing heartbeat. Time seem to stand still, the world fading into insignificance as our desires intertwined.

With hesitant yet eager lips, we embark on a delicate dance, each movement purposeful and tender. Our mouths, like poetic brushstrokes, paint a canvas of emotions—a masterpiece of longing, curiosity, and a hint of trepidation. The touch of our lips is gentle, a feather's caress as if we are cherishing a fragile bloom.

The warmth of her breath mingles with mine, creating an intoxicating symphony of shared anticipation. Our senses heighten, attune to the gentle rhythm of our hearts, as the delicate taste of uncertainty mixes with a potent undercurrent of desire. The world around us ceases to exist, leaving only the exquisite sensations that bound us together in that stolen moment.

Fingers intertwine, a subtle exploration began—a delicate exploration of curves, contours, and the nuances of touch. Every gentle graze of skin against skin ignites a fire within, an electric current that surges through our veins. The electricity flows from the tips of our fingers to the depths of our souls, leaving an indelible mark upon our beings.

Our bodies, in harmony, lean closer, seeking solace and connection. It is a dance of vulnerability, a symphony of surrender, as we allow ourselves to be lost in the enchantment of that single, breath-taking kiss. The world may judge us for this moment of weakness, but in that instant, we know that true strength lay in embracing our desires.

And as we reluctantly part, our lips lingering in a final, tender touch, we know that this fleeting moment would forever be etched in the tapestry of our lives. It is a kiss of shared vulnerability and undeniable passion, a testament to the depths of human connection that could be forged in the face of weakness.

Nivedita is completely out of breath.

As am I.

And painfully aroused.

"Boudoir is just one form of appreciating the woman's body," I say as I trace a line with my index finger on her bare torso.

"Oh, yeah? What else can we do?" she asks in a raspy voice.

"Devouring the body by someone who appreciates it fully," I say. With that, I remove my t-shirt and throw it on the floor while Nivedita undoes my jeans.

In a dance of undeniable attraction, Nivedita and I surrender to the consuming power of passion. As our bodies gravitate closer, a magnetic force draws us into an embrace that transcends the physical realm. The world around us dissolves, leaving only the intoxicating presence of each other.

Our eyes lock, kindling a flame that burned with a fervour previously unknown. In that moment, time seems to lose its hold, granting us the gift of eternity within a single heartbeat. The anticipation hangs thick in the air, charged with electricity, as we delicately brush our lips together, igniting a firestorm of desire.

The taste of her, an exquisite blend of sweetness and warmth, envelopes my senses, intoxicating me further. Our mouths move in synchrony, a tender exploration guided by instinct and yearning. Soft sighs mingled with whispered promises, each breath conveying a depth of emotion that defied words.

As our embrace tighten, hands roam in a delicate ballet of discovery. Fingertips trace the contours of her face, mapping the soft curves with reverence. Our bodies press against each other, moulding into one another's embrace as if seeking solace and completion.

With each stolen moment, the world fades away, leaving only the symphony of our shared desire. The rhythm of our hearts echoed in perfect harmony, our heartbeats synchronized as if we are destined to find each other. The boundaries between our souls blur, and we are consumed by an overwhelming connection that defied reason.

Passion surges like a tempestuous tide, sweeping us away into a realm beyond imagination. We lose ourselves in the sensations, our movements guided by an instinctual longing. The brush of skin against skin set the stage for an intimate ballet, an exploration of pleasure and vulnerability.

Every caress, every whisper, and every stolen breath fuels the flames of desire. Time becomes an ethereal concept, irrelevant in the face of such profound intimacy. The symphony of our passion crescendos, reaching its peak as we indulge in the culmination of our desires—a union that felt like the merging of two souls.

We both scream in pleasure.

And as we reluctantly part, a single thread of connection remain, binding us forever. We emerge from the symphony, breathless and yet profoundly alive, knowing that we have experienced something extraordinary—a transcendent moment of profound intimacy that would forever be etched in the tapestry of our lives.

In the aftermath of our passionate union, as our bodies lay entwined, an overwhelming sense of clarity washes over me. The connection we have forged in this moment of surrender transcends mere desire, evolving into something deeper, something transformative. With my heart racing and filled with a mix of vulnerability and certainty, I find the courage to express the depth of my commitment to Nivedita.

Gazing into her eyes, shimmering with a mixture of passion and vulnerability, I take a deep breath, my voice steady yet laced with emotion.

"Nivedita," I whisper, the words carrying the weight of a lifetime of shared experiences yet to come, "will you marry me?"

The air seems to be still as the question hangs suspended, an unspoken promise of love and devotion. Time stretches out as if waiting for her response, and for a moment, it seems like the world holds its breath. In that fragile space between anticipation and realization, I feel a myriad of emotions collide—a blend of hope, fear, and an unwavering belief in the power of our connection.

Nivedita's eyes widens, reflecting the magnitude of the moment. Her lips trembles, forming a smile that danced with joy and tenderness. As she take my face in her hands, her touch conveys a profound understanding—a recognition that this proposal is not simply born from the intensity of the passion we had shared, but from a deep-rooted love that had blossomed and grown within our souls.

Her voice, a soft melody, filled the air.

"Yes," she whisper, her breath mingling with mine, sealing our fates in a single word. In that instant, the world around us bursts into celebration, as if it had been eagerly awaiting this union, mirroring the jubilant rhythm of our hearts.

We hold each other tightly, cherishing the weight of the moment, knowing that our love had found its purpose and direction. It is a promise of a shared future, a bond that would withstand the tests of time and the trials of life. In that embrace, we embark on a journey as partners, entwined in a love that was both passionate and enduring.

As we lay there, wrapped in each other's arms, the beauty of the moment envelops us—a tapestry woven with vulnerability, desire, and a profound commitment to one another. The world has witnessed our surrender to passion, but it is this proposal that sealed our destiny—an unbreakable bond forged in the fires of love.

Who would have thought that a boudoir photo session would lead to a marriage proposal?

* THE END *

www.ingramcontent.com/pod-product-compliance
Lightning Source LLC
Chambersburg PA
CBHW070312220526
45465CB00004B/1851